Beagles

Dog Books for Kids

By
K. Bennett

Mendon Cottage Books

JD-Biz Publishing

Read More Amazing Animal Books

Purchase at Amazon.com

Table of Contents

Introduction

Chapter 1 Early History

Chapter 2 Fascinating Features & Care

Chapter 3 Amazing Beagle facts

Conclusion A Family's best friend

Author Bio

Introduction

"No matter how little money and how few possessions you own, having a dog makes you rich."

-Louis Sabin

Beagles are beautiful small sized dogs and a member of the hound group. This group of dogs looks similar to the Foxhound, but the design is a bit different.

For example, you will note Beagles have shorter legs and softer ears. And they have a great sense of smell, which makes them efficient in scenting out their target. The word used to describe their hunting skills is "*relentless*," which means they don't give up easily! And this skill has served them well over the years.

Beagles were used mainly for tracking purposes. They would track down animals like deer, rabbits, and other small sized game. And over the years this ability has expanded into other areas. For example today, Beagles are used to detect forbidden agricultural products and other foods, which are not allowed in various countries around the world.

I can personally attest to this fact. When I traveled from London to New Jersey a few years ago, I forgot I had a banana in my bag. A cute little beagle let everyone know, including the officer, that I had forbidden fruit. And she sniffed out my sandwich too! The officers were none too pleased with me, but I couldn't be upset with such a beautiful little tattletale!

For more than 2,500 years Beagle type dogs have existed, but in the 1800's the modern breed we know was born. And now this beautiful dog has become one of the top ten dog breeds in the United States. However, this does not mean Beagles have forgotten their origins!

When it comes to training, Beagles are not the easiest breed to train. Usually, they are so busy following some interesting scent that your commands are left in the dust. So if you decide to have a Beagle as a pet, this part of their personality is something to think about.

Beagles can also be wary of strangers. They are also protective of their family and territorial. So when strangers come around, don't expect your Beagle to say hello! It will take a little time for your pet to warm up before they invite a stranger into the home. Yes, there are exceptions to the rule as with all dog breeds, but this is the standard behavior of a Beagle.

Ultimately Beagles are loyal and faithful companions. Their loving nature and fun personality will endear them to the whole family, but especially children. Full of energy and excitement, Beagles are ready to have fun each and every day! This fun loving spirit makes them an ideal pet for a home with little ones.

Although enigmatic on some occasions, Beagles are certainly recommended as a great household pet. Their highly enthusiastic spirit and intelligence are not only deserving of the title *"man's best friend"* but also… *"Best family friend!"*

Need to get this chewed just right!

 **Chapter 1**

An interesting start – Ancient Greece

Beagles are part of a special family of dogs called hound dogs. Do you know what a hound is? This type of dog is very good at tracking things and will "hound" or pursue a prey until it is caught! This means Beagles are persistent in scenting out objects. And anything that catches their fancy is a potential target. But where did Beagles come from?

Beagle's history is quite ancient… as ancient as Greece. We have to travel back in time near the 5th century. A writer known as Xenophon wrote an interesting book where he talked about a "hound that hunted hares by scent." Ancient Greeks were no strangers to these types of dogs. Hounds were used in the war and even trained to fight. Wealthy women also had hounds as pets and this relationship was stamped on pottery, paintings, coins, etc.

Hounds were also a part of worship. For example the Goddess of hunting known as Artemis is customarily painted with hounds at her side. So the history of this breed is long known, but how do we get to the modern Beagles?

Closer to our time in the 11th century, William the Conqueror brought a beautiful hound known as the Talbot hound to England. During that time these hounds were crossed with Greyhounds to give them a little more speed.

Other crossings bring us to the 18th century where we find the Southern Hound and the Northern Hound. More crossings led to the modern foxhound and then a man known as Reverend Phillip Honeywood put together a Beagle pack in the 1830's. It is generally thought modern Beagles came from this group.

Quite a history, don't you think? But wait…there's more! Phillip Honeywood's Beagles were pure white, so it was left to a man called Thomas Johnson to refine the breed and produce a dog with great hunting skills and a beautiful coat.

There were more refinements over the years, but the basic story of the origin of the Beagle is now set. And in 1885, Beagles were formally accepted as a breed by the American Kennel Club. And today, this lovable dog is considered one of the top ten dog breeds, and its fame has spread around the world.

To think about: Beagles love to have fun, lots of fun and nothing but fun! So, if you are looking for a more passive pet this breed may not be right for you. This desire for fun and boundless energy wrapped in one bundle can be stressful. So before you get a Beagle, weigh the pros and cons of caring for a fun loving pet.

Note of advice: Beagles thrive on a pack relationship. That means you are an inseparable part of the Beagle's life. So if you leave your pet alone for long periods of time, they can get down, upset and suffer from anxiety syndrome. Having this pet requires a level of responsibility, which requires quality time to reassure your pet of your loving attention.

Smell here!

A dog by any other name...

Beagles are great with kids. They love children and are gentle with them. They are well known as fun loving animals, and it when it comes to adventure they are raring to go! So it is important to take care of this aspect of your dog's nature, and make sure it gets adequate exercise to expend their boundless energy.

As noted, this breed is active requiring daily exercise, and their playful personality is very obvious outdoors. They are also great hunters and it is not unusual for them to wander off if they catch "scent" of something. This skill can be a great quality, but it can also be a frustrating experience. Why? Well, when a Beagle catches the "scent" of prey they can follow it for hours if necessary. Even if you try to command them, they may simply ignore you in view of the thrill of the hunt!

The independent attitude of a Beagle then, should be noted. If you decide to run after them trying to get their attention, your Beagle will take it as a sign of more fun...and off they go!

As regards strangers, Beagles take some time to warm up. But once the "ice is broken," they can be extremely affectionate and social. And if they accept you, they will follow you! This trait can display itself with strangers, so this aspect of a Beagles personality needs to be considered. Why? Well if a Beagle befriends a stranger, they may follow them, adding to your frustration.

However, on the upside of this tale, Beagles can howl really well. And they bark loudly and persistently. Their idea is to warn you by any means necessary, so they do whatever it takes.

And if you decide to teach your Beagle to be the perfect pet, you may give up in despair concluding the effort is a waste of time. More than likely your dog will wander off halfway through the training, or the passing of a butterfly will catch its eye!

Important note: Beagles have great hunting skills, so it important to socialize your pet is you have other animals. If you fail to do this and your Beagle sees your pet kitten as prey instead of a companion…you get the idea! Avoid the upset of a Beagle's "present," and ensure that all your pets get along well.

🐾 Chapter 2

Now that you know what Beagles are like and their origins, let us review its features:

In review: Beagles are beautiful dogs with a fun loving personality. They are great companions and thrive in a family pack relationship.

Beagles love being underfoot and they hate being left alone. To ensure the emotional wellbeing of your pet, remember to spend quality time with them. If you need to take care of something and your Beagle will be left on their own for a while, turn on the radio or TV before you leave.

When it comes to behavior, a Beagle's enthusiasm and adventurous spirit will bring a smile to your face and leave you wanting for more. This fun loving nature makes them an ideal companion for children. They are even friendly with other dogs and cats once they are properly socialized. As a whole, Beagles are wonderful companions and a great family pet.

FUN FACTS FOR KIDS: Have you heard of the *Glove* Beagle and the *Pocket* Beagle? What about the *Singing* Beagle? If you are curious and would like to know the differences … ask your parents or a guardian to help you. Then go online and find out what makes each Beagle breed unique!

Looking good

- ***How much can they weigh?*** The male can weigh approximately 22-25 pounds, and the female can weigh approximately 20-23 pounds.

This doesn't mean a Beagle can't weigh more / less than this, but this is the standard weight.

-How tall can they get? Beagles can reach 13-16 inches in height.

-What about babies? Beagle's litters vary. The female can have between 2 -14 puppies. However, the average size is 7 puppies.

-How long to they live? Lifespan is usually between 12 - 15 years.

-What about their coat? Beagles have a hard coat with short hair.

-How often do they shed? Normal shedding is common. However, if you suffer from allergies, this is something to consider.

-What color are they? Beagles have beautiful coats in lustrous tricolor shades. But this is not the only color of the Beagles coat. This variety extends to lemon tones, light tan, reddish tones, browns and even black!

- What about their temperament or personality? As noted previously, Beagles are an amazing breed. And their high intelligence and cheerful personality is a delightful aspect of their personality. They are also great with children and love to play with them.

Wet beagle next to the sea

Caring for your Beagle

Beagles are not only our pets, but also valued members of our home. So we want to be sure they get proper care and like most, if not all of us, the right diet and exercise is important.

Let us begin with the right diet:

Gauging how much your dog should eat is a good place to start. If you notice your pet may be getting a little too heavy (As some Beagles tend to do), cut back on the food intake. If you notice too little weight, then increase the portions of food.

How can you be sure if your dog is being fed correctly? The same principle applies for other breeds, but this general rule of thumb is a nice way to test your animal to see how well you are feeding him.

Try the following test listed on **dogtime.com** at home. Are you ready?

FIRST: Put your thumbs on his spine and run your fingers along the side of the Boxers body.

SECOND: Once there, feel for his ribs beneath the muscle. If you can see them, he needs more food! If you cannot feel them (Too many rolls of fat), you need to put him / her on a diet.

In a Beagles case, just looking at your pet will give you an indication of how well your meal plan is going.

A snack right now would be good :-)

Mealtime

There are lots of choices to feed your Beagles, so it may be hard to choose the best food on the market. These steps (below) will help you make an informed and honest decision regarding the best dog food for your beloved pet. (This advice applies to other breeds as well).

Grrmf.org notes the following recommendations to ensure a happy and healthy pet.

Scratch chemical preservatives: Be on the lookout for ingredients like Ethoxyquin, BHT, BHA, propelyne glycol or sodium nitrates in any form. That includes sodium nitrites too! Instead look for natural preservatives such as Rosemary (herbs), and natural Tocopherols.

Expiration date: Be sure to check the expiration date on the bag. You should purchase food months ahead of this date. Why? Moldy food could be a health factor and you never want to feed your dog this kind of food, which can affect its good health. Usually the bag itself is an indicator. Does it look fresh or do you see grease stains somewhere? Stay away from those unsavory looking bags! Ask the store helpers if you are not sure whether the bag is fresh or not.

A bite of meat: Meat ingredient is a great choice, but be sure it is the FIRST ingredient. This can be Turkey, Lamb or Chicken. Do not buy food with Grain as the first ingredient. Why not? Meat protein is what you are looking for. This is the best nutrition for your pet so search for the meat ingredient as one of the most (if not the most) important in the list. Remember your pet needs animal protein for a beneficial diet.

Avoid animal digest: This is the intestines of other animals! They can contain feet, heads and slaughterhouse waste of other animals. An example as noted at the website is "poultry byproducts."

Sugars and artificial colors: These additives are not healthy or beneficial for your pet so avoid them.

Dog treats: Try to get healthy treats! There are many out there with ingredients that could harm your pet. You could try your hand at making them yourself. Make it family project and have some fun.

The list could go on and on, but you get the idea! Of course if you have the time to make home cooked food for your pet it would be a great alternative to ensure healthy meals.

The website **Beaglepro.com** noted some great tips to help you give the best nutrition to your pet. It also lists the quantities and portions of meals.

The recommended meat ingredients among others are:

Lean chicken
Lamb
Veal
Turkey
Fish

Next are the vegetables.

Sweet potatoes
Carrots
Cauliflower
Potatoes
String beans
Sweet peas
Broccoli

Finish off with an excellent multivitamin or supplement (for dogs) and voila! A well fed, healthy and happy pet.

Note: Not all of us have time to do home cooked meals for our pets, and your pet may not be a fan of vegetables! However, if you decide to purchase commercial dog food, take the time to find the healthiest alternative available and the most nutritious supplements for your pet.

Caution: We all know what foods **NOT** to feed our dogs. You may instantly think of chocolate. But you can add to this list: mushrooms, caffeine, onions, fruit seeds, grapes, raisins and more. If you are unsure of the entire list, look online to see what other foods you need to avoid. And if you are underage, please consult with a parent or guardian before you start your search.

Exercises

Beagles require daily exercise and this can include:

-Breaking a sweat and lots of it!

Beagles are bundles of energy and need constant exercise! So you can jog, run or walk briskly to get their blood flowing. (Note: This is a daily requirement, so if you unable to meet this type of demand on your time, a Beagle may not be the ideal pet for you – If you still want one but need to find other ways to keep the pet happily occupied, talk to a dog trainer or reputable veterinarian for their advice.)

-Running

The best way to keep your Beagle happy is by running your feet off! The more you run the more your Beagle will enjoy the outing. But try to stay away from really hard surfaces. An open field (park area or similar site) is better for its low impact on the frame of your pet. This will help their joints and feet to keep in tip top shape.

- Game of tag or fetch

 Your Beagle will have a wonderful time if you play a game of tag or fetch with them. However, they can get so excited you may soon tire of their boundless enthusiasm. So take it one step at a time and train your pet to understand when playtime is over!

Beagles are great with kids

Living with the family

Children will love having a Beagle as a pet. They are great playmates and will interact with other family pets. Of course to interact with family pets (Like other dogs and cats), there is a degree of socialization required.

In the case of Beagles this will take time, patience and lots of loving attention. Remember Beagles have a highly developed hunting instinct. This means they may see your little kitty not as a pet, but more like prey! To avoid unpleasant results talk to a reputable Veterinarian or animal trainer for the best way to socialize your Beagle.

Beagles enjoy the companionship of their human family, and thrive on loving affection. So be sure to include him / her in your family activities. It is important to note a Beagle's loving affection will put him / her underfoot! So if you do not wish to have the dog constantly at your side, you will have to find other creative ways to occupy their time.

Due to their boundless enthusiasm, Beagles can sometimes go overboard in their loving affection. Perhaps they might knock over a child or scratch them. They could also play bite just for fun. If you are concerned about this behavior, monitor your child during playtimes or teach your Beagle to be a bit less enthusiastic. Remember Beagles are not easy to train, so this will take some time to accomplish. It is wise to take this into account

🐾 Chapter 3

You know I look good!

So, what else can we learn about Beagles? Check out some other details you may like to know.

- A beagle's nose is very sensitive to smell. How sensitive? It has approximately 220 million smell receptors. And yes, you read right. That's million! We, as the human species have approximately 5 million, so it seems the Beagle can smell much better than I can!

- Beagles love to eat, and they eat a lot. So if you decide to hide their treats, don't think your beagle won't find it. And if you don't want to give it to him, he may decide to wrestle you for it!

- When a Beagle is born they are usually black and white. But perhaps you may see some splotches of colors to come. So where does their unique color come from when they are older? Well, as time goes on their color slowly develops into a tan tone, for which they are famous.

- Beagles have a beautiful white tip at the end of their tails. Have you noticed? If not, take a good look. Usually when a Beagle has no white in its tail, it is not considered 100 % purebred. The amount of white does vary from dog to dog, but it should be there somewhere!

-The most famous Beagle that most people know is…SNOOPY from Charles M. Schulz's "Peanuts!" He may have been quiet at the start, but over the years Snoopy has become quite vocal in his thoughts and imagination. Not bad for a little Beagle hmmm?

Twice the fun

FUN FACTS FOR KIDS: Can you guess what the word Beagle means and where it comes from? I will give you a hint: Beagles can be very LOUD…Curious? Then look it up with the help of a parent or guardian online.

Conclusion

Best family friend

In conclusion:

Beagles are a wonderful addition to a family home and the perfect family pet. It is true they can be quite stubborn and independent, but they are also tons of fun!

Beagles are amazing with children and will play with them all day if allowed. Of course on occasion they may get a little excited and knock someone over, but they don't really mean it. This action only reflects the overwhelming happiness they feel to be a part of your life.

If needed, Beagles can get quite loud and are territorial. When it comes to strangers, although wary at first, they can quickly warm up! If you need a good watchdog this trait may not entirely please you, but their affections and boisterous nature outshines most flaws.

More than any other breed, Beagles are fun loving friends. If you decide to make this breed a part of your family home, you could not make a better choice than an outgoing and adorable pet!

Author Bio

K. Bennett is a native from the Island of Roatan, North of Honduras. She loves to write about many different subjects, but writing for children is special to her heart.

Some of her favorite pastimes are reading, traveling and discovering new things. These activities help to fuel her imagination and act like a canvas for more stories.

She also loves fantasy elements like hidden worlds and faraway lands. Basically anything that gets her imagination soaring to new heights!

Her writing credits include local newspaper articles, a writing blog at Wordpress.com and other online stories. It also includes nonfiction books, children books online, and two novellas listed at Amazon.com

Our books are available at

1. Amazon.com

2. Barnes and Noble

3. Itunes

4. Kobo

5. Smashwords

6. Google Play Books

This book is published by

JD-Biz Corp

P O Box 374

Mendon, Utah 84325

http://www.jd-biz.com/

Mendon Cottage Books

P O Box 374, Mendon Utah 84325